Discarded by MVCL

CLASSIC CARS
AN IMAGINATION LIBRARY SERIES

THE STORY OF

# Porsches

Discarded by MVCL

by David K. Wright

MOUNT VERNON CITY LIBRARY
315 Snoqualmie
Mount Vernon, WA 98273-4295
(360) 336-6209

**Gareth Stevens Publishing**
A WORLD ALMANAC EDUCATION GROUP COMPANY

Please visit our web site at: www.garethstevens.com
For a free color catalog describing Gareth Stevens Publishing's
list of high-quality books and multimedia programs,
call 1-800-542-2595 (USA) or 1-800-387-3178 (Canada).
Gareth Stevens Publishing's fax: (414) 332-3567.

Library of Congress Cataloging-in-Publication Data

Wright, David K.
    The story of Porsches / by David K. Wright.
      p. cm. — (Classic cars: an imagination library series)
    Includes bibliographical references and index.
    Summary: Surveys the history of the Porsche automobile and its designs,
engines, and performance.
    ISBN 0-8368-3193-4 (lib. bdg.)
    1. Porsche automobiles—Juvenile literature. [1. Porsche automobiles—
History.]  I. Title.
TL215.P75W75   2002
629.222'2—dc21                    2002021777

First published in 2002 by
**Gareth Stevens Publishing**
A World Almanac Education Group Company
330 West Olive Street, Suite 100
Milwaukee, WI 53212 USA

Text: David K. Wright
Cover design and page layout: Scott M. Krall
Series editor: Jim Mezzanotte
Picture Researcher: Diane Laska-Swanke

Photo credits: Cover, pp. 7, 9, 17, 19, 21 © Ron Kimball; pp. 5, 11, 15 © Richard Adams;
p. 13 Courtesy of Tweeks

This edition © 2002 by Gareth Stevens, Inc. All rights reserved to Gareth Stevens, Inc. No part
of this book may be reproduced, stored in a retrieval system, or transmitted in any form or by any
means, electronic, mechanical, photocopying, recording, or otherwise without the prior written
permission of the publisher except for the inclusion of brief quotations in an acknowledged review.

Printed in the United States of America

2 3 4 5 6 7 8 9 06 05 04

*Front cover:* Like most Porsches, this 1965 model has its engine in the rear. Porsches are famous for their speed and handling.

# TABLE OF CONTENTS

Words that appear in the glossary are printed in **boldface** type the first time they occur in the text.

# THE FIRST PORSCHES

Ferdinand Porsche wanted to make a car with his name on it. All his life, the German **engineer** had **designed** cars for other companies. In 1948, Ferdinand Porsche's small factory began building the car of his dreams — a sports car.

This new car was small. It had a smooth, rounded body. Years earlier, Porsche had designed the famous Volkswagen "Beetle." His new car used the engine and other parts from the Volkswagen Beetle. Like the Beetle, its engine was in the rear.

Ferdinand Porsche finished 355 projects for other companies before making his own automobile. He named his new car Model 356!

This 1949 Model 356 Porsche has been turned into a racing car. Early Porsches used many parts from the Volkswagen Beetle.

To help sell its new cars, the Porsche company entered them in auto races in Europe. At first, the company used a 356 model that it **modified** for racing. Then the company built a car just for racing. It was called the 550 Spyder.

Porsche Spyders did very well in racing events all over Europe. They were fast and reliable, and they often finished ahead of cars that were much larger and more powerful. Because Porsches ran so well, many drivers wanted to race them.

# CRAZY ABOUT PORSCHES

In the 1950s, sports cars **imported** from Europe became popular in the United States. Along with Jaguars, MGs, and other European cars, Porsches sold very well. Porsches cost a lot, but they were well built. People who could afford expensive cars did not mind paying a lot for a Porsche.

Porsches became known for being reliable and fun to drive. They were not as powerful as some other sports cars, but they could be driven very fast on curving roads. James Dean was a famous Hollywood actor who owned a Porsche. In 1955, he drove his Porsche too fast and died in an accident.

*In the 1950s, the small, fast Porsches became popular in the United States. Many Porsches, such as this 1957 Speedster, were convertibles.*

# FUN WITH THE 911

In 1963, the Porsche company began selling a new model called the 911. Like the 356, the 911 had its engine in the back. But it had a more **streamlined** body and a new, more powerful engine. The 911 Targa was a convertible model that became popular.

It was easy to feel like a skilled driver in such a quick, solid car. Some people had problems because they drove too fast. They seemed to think they did not have to obey speed limits! Most Porsche owners **maintained** their cars very well, and some never drove their cars in rain or snow.

*This 1968 Porsche 912 Targa is a less expensive version of the 911. It has a removable roof and a bar for protection in case of an accident.*

Porsches were sleek and fast and a lot of fun to drive, but they were also expensive. In 1969, Porsche began selling a new, lower-priced model that more people could afford.

The new model was called the 914. The 914 was smaller than the 911 and had only two seats. It did not have its engine far in the back, like the 911. Instead, the 914 was a **mid-engine** car. Its engine was right behind the seats.

The 914 was fast and handled well, but many people thought it was ugly. Some said they could not tell which end of the car was the front and which end was the back!

*The Porsche 914 had a removable top, and its engine was right behind the seats. Many people thought the car looked strange, but it handled well.*

# 1,000 HORSEPOWER!

Over the years, Porsche kept making racing cars. One of the company's most successful racing cars was the Porsche 917. This car had a twelve-cylinder engine that produced 1,000 **horsepower**. With this engine, the 917 could reach a speed of 240 miles (386 kilometers) an hour!

In the 1970s, the Porsche 917 competed in a popular racing series called the Canadian-American Challenge Cup, or "Can-Am." The 917 was soon beating the other Can-Am cars. In 1973, all the races in the series were won by a Porsche 917!

*The Porsche 917 has a smooth, lightweight body. Its huge, powerful engine is located right behind the driver's head!*

© Richard Adams

# HIGH SPEED

Engineers at Porsche worked on improving the company's cars. In the 1970s, for example, Porsche introduced the 911 Turbo. This special 911 had a **turbocharger** that made its engine much more powerful, so it was very fast. The Turbo could reach a speed of 150 miles (240 km) an hour!

Porsche also began building other models that had their engines in the front. It added a turbocharger to one of these front-engine models, too. By the 1990s, Porsche was selling many different models, including special 911 convertibles. All of these Porsches were fast!

This 1989 Porsche is a special 911 convertible called the Speedster. It can reach a speed of well over 100 miles (160 km) an hour.

# BETTER AND BETTER

Today, Porsche still makes a version of the 911. The car has been around for more than thirty-five years! The 911 has gone through many changes, because Porsche engineers have always tried to come up with new **innovations** for the car.

In 1988, Porsche began building a 911 that had four-wheel drive. With four-wheel drive, power from the engine goes to all four wheels. Now the 911 could zoom around corners, even in terrible weather.

Four-wheel drive comes in handy during a **rally** through the woods. Muddy dirt roads are no match for Porsches with four-wheel drive!

*This latest Porsche 911 is the Carrera model. It is available with either two-wheel drive or four-wheel drive.*

In 1996, Porsche came out with a new sports car called the Boxster. It was a two-seat, mid-engine convertible. The Boxster looked a lot like the old Porsche Spyder from the 1950s.

The Boxster is just one of the many cars that Porsche builds today. Some of the cars are meant to be driven on the street, and some are strictly for the race track. They all have a **reputation** for being fast and reliable.

Over fifty years have passed since Ferdinand Porsche first created a car with his name on it. But today, Porsche is still going strong!

# MORE TO READ AND VIEW

**Books (Nonfiction)**
*Big Book of Race Cars.* Trevor Lord (DK Publishing)
*Porsche. Ultimate Cars* (series). A. T. McKenna (Abdo & Daughters)
*The Porsche 911.* Michael Burgan (Capstone Press)
*The World's Most Exotic Cars.* John Martin (Capstone Press)

**Videos (Nonfiction)**
*The Distinguished Racing Heritage of Porsche.*
   (Brentwood Home Video)
*Porsche 911.* (A&E)
*Porsche Story.* (White Star)

**Videos (Fiction)**
*Le Mans.* (Paramount Studios)

# PLACES TO WRITE AND VISIT

Here are three places to contact for more information:

**Automotive Hall of Fame**
21400 Oakwood Blvd.
Dearborn, MI 48124
USA
1-313-240-4000
www.automotive
halloffame.org

**Porsche Collection**
Porschestrasse 42
Zuffenhausen 7000
Germany
0711-82031

**Tweeks**
P.O. Box 1368
Effingham, IL 62401
USA
1-888-489-3357
www.madirect.com

# WEB SITES

Web sites change frequently, but we believe the following web sites are going to last. You can also use good search engines, such as **Yahooligans!** [**www.yahooligans.com**] or **Google** [**www.google.com**], to find more information about Porsches. Here are some keywords to help you: *Boxster, Ferdinand Porsche, Porsche 356, Porsche 911, Porsche 914,* and *Porsche 917.*

**www.geocities.com/MotorCity/
7124/porsche.htm**
This web site is called *Dan Hlavacek's Porsche Page.* The site has a lot of pictures of different Porsches.

**pages.prodigy.com/XporscheX/
porsche.htm**
Visit this web site to see pictures of the 911, Boxster, and other Porsche models. This site is called *Porsche: There Is No Substitute.*

**www.porsche.com/english/company/**
This site is the official web site of Porsche. Visit this site to see pictures of Ferdinand Porsche and learn about all the different models the Porsche company has made over the years, including its latest models.

**www.v-zweeden.com/ned.htm**
Take the Porsche history tour! This site has dozens of photos of every single Porsche model, from the first 356 models to the models Porsche makes today.

# GLOSSARY

You can find these words on the pages listed. Reading a word in a sentence helps you understand it even better.

**designed** (de-ZINED) — created the plans needed to build something 4

**engineer** (ehn-jin-EAR) — a person who plans the construction of buildings or machines 4, 16, 18

**horsepower** (HORS-pow-ur) — a unit of measurement for an engine's power, based on the amount of weight one horse can pull 14

**imported** (im-PORT-ed) — brought in from another country 8

**innovations** (in-oh-VAY-shunz) — better products or ways of doing things 18

**maintained** (mane-TAYND) — took care of something on a regular basis so it stayed in good condition 10

**mid-engine** (MID-EN-gin) — having the engine in the middle, behind the seats but ahead of the rear wheels 12

**modified** (MOD-if-eyed) — made changes to something 6

**rally** (RAL-eeh) — an auto race that travels over very rough roads 18

**reputation** (REP-you-TAY-shun) — what people think of a person or thing 20

**streamlined** (STREEM-lined) — having a rounded shape that moves easily through the air 10

**turbocharger** (TUR-boe-char-jur) — a machine that uses an engine's exhaust gases to help the engine produce more power 16

# INDEX

**24**

MOUNT VERNON CITY LIBRARY